Anne Ward was born in Listowel and lived in Ballyduff until her family moved to Galway. She was educated in the Dominican College, Taylor's Hill. Ann then worked in Germany and later returned to Ireland and she worked in Clonmel and Kanturk. Ann now lives in Mallow with her husband James and two children. She gives courses on microwave cookery throughout the country together with training courses for electrical sales people and private groups. Her other book *The Irish Microwave Cook Book* is also published by the Mercier Press.

GW00598660

MICROWAVE COOKING
FOR ALL OCCASIONS

ANN WARD

MERCIER PRESS

Mercier Press
PO Box 5, 5 French Church Street, Cork
16 Hume Street, Dublin 2

© Ann Ward

ISBN 1 85635 095 7

A CIP is available of this book from the British Library.

10 9 8 7 6 5 4 3 2 1

To my parents
Dr Michael and Lucy Sweeney
and also
my husband James and our children
Laura and Brian

The support of the ESB is gratefully acknowledged

Printed in Ireland by Colour Books

Contents

Introduction

Microwave cookery is here to stay. Microwave ovens were first invented in 1947 and are a terrific way of saving time and electricity.

As my first book, *The Irish Microwave Cookbook*, proved so popular that it went to reprint after the first three weeks, I thought there was a great opening for a microwave cookbook dealing mainly with festive cooking and different ways of using left-over turkey and ham. You will not realise that you are having turkey or ham so often with the choice of recipes I have given here.

Microwave cooking is economical on electricity and very energy efficient. The cooking time is reduced by the cooking process and there is no preheating with a microwave, it actually starts to cook as soon as it is turned on.

Christmas Day, in particular, should be a relaxing day. To ensure this, preparation in advance for the main meal is essential. The ham can be cooked the day before and the turkey can be cooked on Christmas morning, which leaves plenty of time to cook all the vegetables. These can be cooked in separate containers on the turntable while the turkey is continuing to cook during the standing time.

As the plum pudding only takes three minutes to reheat, there is no need to have the pudding steaming for hours, creating condensation in the kitchen and wasting electricity. You can reheat the pudding when the family want to eat it – they are usually too full after the Christmas meal to enjoy the plum pudding directly after.

I have also continued with some more hints and tips which I hope will be of interest to you. As with my previous book, all the following recipes are based on a 700 watt microwave cooker.

I am looking forward to meeting as many of you as possible while giving microwave cookery demonstrations or lessons throughout the country.

I hope you will enjoy this book as much as my first – *The Irish Microwave Cookbook.*

ANN WARD

Microwave Information and Handy Tips

1. Never turn on the microwave without having something in it – i.e., a cup of water – otherwise you will damage your microwave.

2. Read the manufacturers *Book of Instructions*.

3. Become familiar with the dials on your microwave initially by reheating and defrosting. Then try out recipes.

4. Always stir a cup of boiling water before adding tea/coffee or it will overflow due to lack of oxygen. Always taste anything reheated in a cup with a spoon as it is impossible to determine the temperature of the contents by feeling the outside of the cup. The microwaves concentrate on heating the contents of your dish/cup therefore you are able to handle the cup without the use of oven gloves.

5. Do not coat meat, chicken, etc, with beaten egg as this forms a seal like a skin and will burst.

6. Always prick the skin of tomatoes, apples, peppers and potatoes and the yolks of eggs otherwise the skin will burst and spatter the contents in the oven.

7. If you have a jar of honey which has crystallised, remove the lid, place the jar in the oven and microwave on Medium (50%) for two minutes.

8. If reheating a scone or pastry based product, place a piece of kitchen paper underneath otherwise the base will get soggy from the condensation.

9. Condensation is normal in the microwave. To eliminate it after cooking either leave the door open for a few minutes or wipe with a piece of kitchen paper.

10. When cooking fatty foods like chicken, place a sheet of kitchen paper over the breast to prevent spatters hitting the top of the oven which will require cleaning afterwards.

11. When reheating meals on plates, it is better to cover with kitchen paper, as cling film, unless vented by turning back one side, will create steam and make your meal soggy.

12. Pyrex is ideal for using in the microwave. The lids are loose enough to allow steam to escape and the range of sizes is ideal for family meals.

13. Never use gold or silver rimmed cups/plates/dishes, etc, in the microwave as they will reflect the microwaves back into the magnetron and cause damage. The same applies to silver ties which come with freezer bags, cooking bags, etc. Also never use foil trays which come with frozen pies, apple pies, etc.

14. If you leave you cup of tea/coffee out of your hand and forget about it – reheat it for 30 seconds and it will taste exactly as it did when you made it.

15. Jelly can be dissolved without adding water. Just microwave for 45 seconds. Then you can add cold water gradually, stirring continuously thereby reducing the setting time.

16. When defrosting, leave the wrapping on the product – i.e., plastic bag. The bag will not melt.

17. You do not have to defrost peas/green beans/ Brussel sprouts, etc, before cooking. You can also place the quantities you require in freezer bags with very little water and cook several types of vegetable at once. This is very convenient if you have children with different tastes, whereas before you could not cook several different vegetables in different saucepans because of lack of space on the hob.

18. When calculating times of recipes against your own wattage of your microwave, follow this simple guideline:
If your microwave is 800 watts and the recipe you are following is for 700 watts, deduct 1 minute per 100 watts.

If on the other hand the recipe is for 800 watts and your oven is 700 watts then you add a minute to the cooking time as your oven would cook slower than the 800 watt.

19. If you use cheap stewing beef with a lot of sinew it will turn out tough as the microwave will concentrate on the sinew. Trim fat and sinew off stewing beef before cooking. Remember that microwaves cook quickly so they do not have the time to soften tough pieces of meat.

20. If cooking large pieces of meat – roast beef, lamb, bacon – I would recommend the purchase of a temperature probe. This will tell you the inside temperature of the meat and you will be able to judge when it will be cooked more precisely.

21. When cooking bacon, I would recommend you cook it in a casserole dish with the lid on as bacon spatters a lot. Do not take any notice of the spattering sounds as it is only fat bursting.

22. *Browning:* As microwaves do not brown food, the following suggestions may be helpful:

a) Magic cooking bags will colour your chicken/roast, etc.

b) Schwartz microwave seasoning can be shaken on top of the roast.

c) Paprika sprinkled on top gives a rich colour.

d) Bisto and a little water mixed to a smooth paste and brushed on works very well.

e) Soy sauce and vegetable oil or breadcrumbs sprinkled on top.

f) In the case of puddings/sponges, chocolate and coffee flavours are ideal. Alternatively chocolate/coffee toppings.

23. If your kitchen paper blows off whatever you are cooking, just wet it a little with a drop of water and this will weigh it down sufficiently.

24. When reheating a scone, 15 seconds is enough time as it has already been cooked. Remember to place the scone on a piece of kitchen paper to avoid the base going soggy.

25. Fish cooks very quickly in the microwave. A normal fillet of plaice/cod/whiting will only take two minutes, a full trout will take 4 minutes. Be careful as it is very easy to overcook fish.

26. Always cook for the least number of minutes recommended in the recipe. You can always continue to cook for another 30 seconds but it is very easy to overcook when microwaving.

27. Herbs can be dried in the microwave. Place your herbs between two sheets of kitchen paper and microwave on high for three minutes or until dry and flaky. Rub the sheets of kitchen paper together and store herbs in an airtight container.

28. Flowers can also be dried in a microwave. However, if you 'overcook' them, they will flake just like herbs.

29. Always keep your microwave clean otherwise the microwaves will concentrate on the dirt which will throw out your cooking times.

30. Sauces, soups, custards, etc, come out perfectly when made in a microwave. You do not get the lumps as you would on the normal hob if you do not continue to stir.

31. *Browning dish:* This is the only container which you can place in a microwave empty and turn on the microwave. Usually the browning dish is heated in the microwave for five minutes approximately. Then you remove it from the microwave. The dish will be hot so use oven gloves. The heat in the dish will brown your chops, rashers, sausages, etc, but if you want to cook six chops for example remember that the dish is cooling down while you are using it. Place 3 chops in the dish, wait for 30 seconds, turn and remove. Put in the second lot, turn and remove as above. If the dish cools down you will have to reheat it again for another 5 minutes before continuing. *However it is very important to follow the instruc-*

tions given with your own type of browning dish.

32. *Stacking frame:* This is ideal where you have two or three children arriving at one time for lunch/dinner. Stack your meals and reheat them at the same time. If you find one is cooler than the others, stop half way during cooking and rotate dishes.

33. *Poached eggs:* You can get an accessory which holds water underneath and the eggs – up to five – sit in cups on top. A similar type of product was brought out previously as an attachment for a frying pan. Remember to pierce the yolks of eggs before cooking.

34. *Boiled eggs:* It is better not to try these in your microwave as you could cause damage if the egg bursts. They can be cooked on defrost for five minutes but I would not recommend it. Accessories can also be purchased for egg boiling. Personally I would stick to the hob method of boiling eggs.

35. One accessory which is very handy is the meat tray. It has slits for the meat juice to go through and the tray underneath collects the juice. Ideal for carving later or to pour the juice for using in gravy. It is also very good for cooking chicken as this contains a lot of fat.

36. Cocoa is lovely out of a microwave. Put your cocoa into your mug, add sugar, a little milk and stir until blended. Fill the mug with cold milk and microwave on high for 1¹/₂ minutes. Stop once during cooking to stir.

37. Baked potatoes are very easy in a microwave. Pierce the skin about four times with a fork and cook on high for four minutes. Two potatoes would take about six minutes, three potatoes would take about eight minutes. Try to have potatoes of an even size. Large quantities of potatoes would not save time in the microwave but ideal for small quantities. You can also cut slits on the top of the potatoes and put cheese in these. Not only do they look good but they taste great.

38. The microwave is very economical on electricity as the cooking time is reduced by the cooking process. As I said in my Introduction there is no preheating with a microwave, it actually starts to cook as soon as it is turned on.

Example of cooking times:

1 large chicken – Normal oven – $1^1/2$ hours

1 large chicken – Microwave – 20 minutes

39. By using a microwave you automatically have less washing up. You can have scrambled egg, boiled milk, porridge at any time you like and you can serve in the dish which it has been cooked in. No dirty saucepans to clean. Many of the recipes can be cooked on the dish in which it is served which will cut down on wash up.

40. Circular dishes are better to use as microwaves concentrate on an angle too much thereby overcooking at the corners.

41. *Standing time:* This is important when cooking a joint of meat, turkey, large thick stew, etc.

The food continues to cook after the oven has been turned off. In the case of a large joint of meat you would require a standing time of possibly twenty minutes. You remove the meat from the microwave and cover with tin foil to retain the heat while it finishes cooking. While this is going on, take this time to cook your vegetables or dessert. You will be surprised how quickly the time goes. In the event of cooking a chicken, you will find that the time has elapsed by the time you have served the accompanying vegetables on the plates.

There is no need to think about standing time in the case of light products like eggs, fish, light puddings, custards, sauces, etc.

42. When purchasing bowls look for those which are

microwave proof as there is little or no difference in the price. Everyone has plenty of suitable dishes at home for the microwave without going out especially to buy some. Be careful of using plastic and make sure the plastic you use is suitable for a microwave.

43. Bread baskets and wooden boards can be used for very short periods of time in the microwave. If used over a long period they will dry out.

44. When cooking straight from the freezer remember to defrost meat first. Also, home made pies with a large quantity of meat need to be defrosted before cooking.

45. It is better not to use salt/pepper to season prior to cooking as the taste is much stronger after microwaving. Add these after cooking.

46. Do not add too much milk when scrambling eggs. I recommend 1 tablespoon of milk per egg.

47. Rice cooks perfectly and will not stick when cooked in a microwave, but does not cook faster than the conventional method. Again no dirty saucepans.

48. Use microwave cling film only. Do not use the standard cling film. If you find that the microwave cling film tears when you try to slit it, cover the dish, then double back one edge which will suffice.

49. If you are using a combination oven/microwave remember that you cannot use plastic when operating the conventional oven. Also the dishes will get hot when using the conventional oven. Again you must be careful when using the grill and make sure you do not use a container which will melt. Pyrex is ideal in these instances. Use oven gloves.

50. Use very little water when cooking vegetables. One or two tablespoons will be sufficient. Always slit the stalk of broccoli or cauliflower before cooking to ensure even cooking. The nutrients are retained in vegetables as they are cooked quickly and you are not pouring them down the drain when straining.

51. *Turntable:* This is to distribute the microwaves evenly during cooking. Even though you have a turntable you will still have to stir the contents occasionally.

52. If you do not have a turntable you will have to stop the cooking process and rotate the dish inside. One advantage of not having a turntable is to be able to cook a leg of lamb, leg of pork or a turkey as the legs will not get caught when trying to rotate on the turntable. Again you will have to rotate to ensure even cooking.

53. *Stirrer Fan:* This is instead of a turntable. The fan rotates from the ceiling of the oven thereby circulating the microwaves.

54. *Grill:* This can be handy in a microwave but the grill element is usually 1,000 watts, sometimes 1,300 watts. The grill on a conventional cooker is 2,000 watts so it will take longer to grill something on the grill in a microwave cooker. They are ideal for colouring food which you have already microwaved.

55. Because microwaves cook much faster than the normal method of cooking, smells, as in that of cauliflower, are greatly reduced.

56. Increase the juice from citrus fruits by heating for 40 seconds before squeezing.

57. Never block the vents at sides/back or top of your oven.

58. Always open lids of casseroles away from your face as steam builds up inside and could burn you.

59. Do not rinse the turntable in water straight after cooking or it could crack. Leave it stand for 20 minutes.

60. If you leave out something from the ingredients, remember to reduce your cooking time.

61. Cooking times may vary a little as the cooking times will depend on the density of the items being cooked and each oven will vary in capacity, size and wattage. You must try the recipes given and adjust accordingly. This will come with practice and time.

62. Never heat alcohol as in making a hot whiskey. You may heat the water and sugar, then add the whiskey. If you try to heat the whiskey on its own it could ignite. In some recipes you will be asked to heat alcohol for 30 seconds at the low setting. This is acceptable.

63. When making hot whiskey do not put the slice of lemon into the water when you are heating it as the taste of lemon increases to such an extent that the taste of lemon will eliminate the taste of alcohol.

64. Microwave cookers are ideal for anyone who has difficulty in bending down to take a roasting dish from the conventional oven. Being at table top height they make the transfer of dishes into and out of the oven safe and easy to handle.

65. Microwave cookers are portable. You can use them on the patio when barbecuing to reheat what has already been cooked on the barbecue or you can take them on holidays with you if you are renting a house or going to a mobile home. On holidays you do not want to have to go back to the time-consuming way of preparing a meal.

66. When cleaning your microwave cooker abrasive cleaners are not to be used. Regular cleaning with warm water and a cloth will suffice.

67. Remember that leaded crystal cannot be used in the microwave because of the lead content.

68. Meat should be at room temperature before cooking for best results.

69. To peel tomatoes place 2 cups of boiling water in

bowl or jug, add the two tomatoes and heat on high for 1 minute or until the skin splits. Plunge tomatoes into cold water and then you can peel the tomatoes easily.

70. Tear free onions. Trim the ends off the onion, place on a paper towel, heat on high for 30 seconds. Remove skin and chop/slice or whatever.

71. Refresh crackers or biscuits by placing on double layer of paper towel, cook on high for one minute, let them stand for 2–3 minutes and they will be perfectly dry and crispy again.

72. If you find there is a smell in your microwave after cooking curry, chilli, fish, etc, deodorise your oven by placing a cup of warm water with a slice or two of lemon in it into your oven and microwave for 2–3 minutes.

73. Recycled paper towels are not suitable for microwave use as there could be particles of metal contained in them.

74. Use glass containers not plastic when cooking foods which contain a high sugar content as sugar gets very hot and could melt some types of plastic.

75. You can shield food with small amounts of aluminium foil to avoid overcooking, i.e., poultry wings, turkey legs or the tail of fish.

76. If you have a combination microwave with grill and oven please use oven gloves at all times as you can easily forget that when using the grill or convection oven the dishes will get hot.

77. If you are using stock cubes just cover the cube with cold water and microwave on high for 1 minute. Stir to blend cube with water.

78. To colour chops a mixture of soy sauce and vegetable oil is a good combination. Just brush on, then microwave in the normal way.

79. If you like frozen pizzas, frozen pies, etc, a browning dish would be essential for you. You heat the browning dish first, then place the pizza on the dish and microwave for 2 minutes. This ensures that the base of the pizza does not go soggy. Remember to remove the foil dish under the pies.

80. Sliced pineapple rings (unsweetened) or corn niblets added to rice make a great salad.

81. When making jelly, add syrup from peaches/pears, etc, which you may have left over after making a flan.

82. You can not bake directly on the glass turntable, i.e., to make quiche. You must bake the pastry in another dish which is to be placed on top of the glass turntable.

83. Plates can be heated in a microwave by placing wet sheets of kitchen paper between the plates and the microwave for 2 minutes.

84. Unless stated – do not cover dishes in the following recipes.

85. Never use a butter carton to melt butter as the plastic is too soft and will melt.

86. Microwaves are ideal for melting butter for making stuffing. You can melt it in the dish in which you are making the stuffing.

87. *Covering food:* If you need the steam to help you cook/heat, then you cover the food, e.g., vegetables, soups, casseroles. These require steam as well as microwaves to help cook and thereby reduce cooking times. Foods which are covered in breadcrumbs or which require a dry top should not be covered, e.g., omelette, chicken kiev, bread and butter pudding.

88. The lids of pyrex dishes can be ideal for baking apple tarts, etc.

89. Do not use foam containers in which you get bunburgers from a take away.

90. If you want to tie a plastic bag an elastic band is ideal. It will not heat or cook and will be just the same as before use.

91. Cocktail sticks and wooden skewers can be used to tie a stuffed chicken, chicken kiev, cabbage rolls, or the wooden skewers can be used on the barbecue and reheated in the microwave when the guests arrive.

92. When cooking rashers use a meat rack with slits through which the fat falls. Cover with kitchen paper. Remember to snip rind with kitchen scissors to avoid curling.

93. For a simple hot syrup place 30ml/2 tablespoons of dark sugar in a bowl with 28 g/1 oz butter and cook on high for 2 minutes. Ideal topping for ice cream but remember to pour on just before serving as it will melt the ice cream.

94. Coloured kitchen paper is usually not recommended as the colours could go on food while cooking. You can use a coloured kitchen paper if you either wrap or cover food with the white side.

95. Cheese gets stringy when overcooked so remember to heat gently.

96. To reheat rice add 1 tablespoon water and cover. Cook on high for 2–3 minutes.

97. Fondue parties are made very simple with the help of your microwave. The cheese can be popped in and reheated at regular intervals.

98. To test for jam setting, place a small spoonful of jam on a saucer and allow to become cold. If it wrinkles when pushed with a finger, setting point has been reached.

99. To sterilise jars, half fill with water and heat until boiling. Pour off the water and drain for a short time before filling.

100. It is important to stir during cooking as microwaves cook from the outside in. You will see this clearly when microwaving an omelette or minced beef. As the microwaves do not cook evenly, it is important to stir food every two minutes. Remember, cooking times in the microwave are very short.

101. If you make your sauce in a measuring jug it is easy to pour.

102. To test if your favourite mug or dish is microwave proof fill the cup to one-third and heat on high for 30 seconds. If the cup/dish is cool and the water warm, it is microwave proof. If however, the water is cold and the dish is warm, it is not suitable for microwave use. Remember, microwaves cook what is in the container, not the container.

103. Peel mandarin oranges into strips 1 inch (2.5 cm). Lay out on kitchen paper. Microwave on high for 5–6 minutes until crisp. Turn over halfway through cooking. Use crumbled in chocolate sauce or ice cream.

104. If your make-up has hardened in your tube, remove the cap and microwave on high for 15 seconds.

105. To ensure that your plum pudding falls out perfectly, line the bowl with microwave cling film or grease proof paper.

106. For a quick sauce to top ice-cream, heat 3 tablespoons of raspberry jam for 30 seconds

107. To soften brown sugar, place sugar in a microwave proof dish, add one slice of apple or one slice of bread cover and microwave on high for 25–30 seconds.

108. To melt chocolate, place in casserole dish, microwave on high for 2–3 minutes, stir every minute.

109. To prove bread dough, place dough in microwave proof dish. Place cup of very hot water alongside the dish, cover the dough with kitchen paper. Microwave on low – 10% for 20–25 minutes.

110. If you like weak tea, pour two cups for yourself, you can reheat the second cup when you want it, as it will not get any stronger.

111. Keep your sliced pan in the freezer and take out the amount you require for lunch time sandwiches. Four slices will defrost in 1.5 minutes. Remember to place the bread on a sheet of kitchen paper. You will have fresh bread every day.

112. *To dry flowers:* You can buy silica gel from a florist wholesaler. Pour the gel, which is salt-like, into a cardboard-box, a shoe-box is ideal. The reason for using a cardboard box is because any moisture will be absorbed by the cardboard. Cover the base of the box to a depth of 2 inches/5 cm Cut the flower stems about 1 inch/2.5 cm from the head. Place flowers into gel so that the heads do not touch each other. Cover the heads with a layer of silica gel. Place container in microwave and replace cover. For 6–8 flowers, allow 3 minutes on high. It is very important not to disturb the box until the following day. Remove the stems very carefully and if they do not seem dry, microwave them for another minute. At this stage you will require a tin with a tight-fitting lid, a biscuit tin is ideal. Shake some of the silica gel on the base of the tin, gently remove the flower stems, place them in the gel in the tin with their heads up. Keep the flowers in this container for about five days. When you remove the flowers it is essential that you brush the flowers with a soft brush to remove any remaining gel. Use floral tape to bind the flower to a piece of wire.

The silica gel can be reused for years. If you see blue crystals in the silica gel it is caused by excessive moisture. This can be rectified by heating in the microwave for 2–3 minutes – again, use a cardboard box for this.

113. To toast nuts – almonds, coconut, etc. Place evenly on plate. Microwave on high for 3–4 minutes. Stir every minute.

114. When rolling out small amounts of pastry, place dough between two sheets of cling-film. This will keep your surface clean and make it easy to transfer to dish.

115. You can adjust the timer at any time without causing damage. If you set the timer for 4 minutes, then realise it should have only been set for 2 minutes, just reset the dial. You can also open the door at any time to stir the contents.

116. If you have someone confined to bed, it is possible to have a microwave at their bedside so that they can reheat a meal or make a hot drink for themselves.

117. It is normal for steam to escape from the vents. That is what the vents are there for.

118. To cook no-soak marofat peas, place peas in a casserole dish, cover with boiling water, cover dish and microwave on high for 2–3 minutes.

119. To dry out damp salt, pour salt into a small bowl, microwave on high for 1 minute – and you will have perfectly dry salt!

120. To sterilise earth for growing tomatoes, etc., place 448 g/1 lb of earth in a plastic bag and microwave on high for 4 minutes.

121. Sand for use in play-schools can be sterilised as above.

STARTERS

Chicken Liver Pate

224 g chicken livers trimmed and sliced (8 oz)
224 g streaky rashers chopped (8 oz)
56 g mushrooms sliced (2 oz)
1 onion finely chopped
112 g butter (4 oz)
1 teaspoon mixed herbs (5 ml)
2 tablespoons brandy (30 ml)
1 clove garlic finely chopped or crushed
Freshly ground black pepper

Place butter, herbs, garlic and pepper in casserole dish and microwave on high for 45 seconds to melt butter. Add chicken liver, rashers, onion and mushrooms, cover and microwave on high for 8 minutes – stir every two minutes. Put liver mixture and brandy in food processor or liquidiser and blend until smooth. Pour into greased ramekin dishes and cook for 10 minutes. Pour a little melted butter over to seal each dish.

Stuffed Aubergine

336 g sausage meat (12 oz)
1 large aubergine
1 onion finely chopped
56 g sliced mushrooms (2 oz)
28 g fresh breadcrumbs (1 oz)
1 teaspoon Worcestershire sauce (5 ml)
$^1/_4$ teaspoon dried basil (1.2 ml)
75 ml water (3 fl oz)

56 g grated cheddar cheese (2 oz)

Place sausage meat in large casserole dish, cover and micro-wave on high for 4–5 minutes, stir twice during cooking time. Drain.

Cut aubergine lengthways, trim off stalk and scoop out flesh.

Chop the flesh and place in bowl with the onion. Micro-wave for 3–4 minutes. Add sausage meat, mushrooms, breadcrumbs, Worcestershire sauce, basil and seasoning. Fill shells with stuffing. Pour water into large dish, place shells on top, cover and microwave for 5 minutes. When cooked sprinkle grated cheese on top – the heat from the stuffing will melt the cheese.

PRAWN STUFFED COURGETTES

2 courgettes
168 g frozen prawns (6 oz)

Wine Sauce
56 g butter (2 oz)
75 ml white wine (3 fl oz)
2 tablespoons lemon juice (30 ml)
1 tablespoon sugar (15 ml)
1 tablespoon cornflour (15 ml)

Place prawns in dish, cover and defrost for 2 minutes or until defrosted. In large casserole dish melt butter on high for 30 seconds. Slice courgette into 2 inch chunks, scoop out centre with spoon leaving a little flesh on bottom to hold the sauce.

Blend cornflour in a cup with a little wine, add to melted butter with remaining wine, courgette flesh, lemon juice and sugar.

Cook on high for 2-3 minutes until the sauce is thick. Add prawns and microwave on high for a further two minutes. Pour sauce into hollowed courgettes. Place in circle in large dish and microwave on high for 2 minutes.

Smoked Salmon Parcels

1 cucumber
2 tablespoons soured cream (30 ml)
3 tablespoons mayonnaise (45 ml)
Juice half lemon
1 tablespoon dried basil (15 ml)
224 g smoked salmon (8 oz)
Lemon slices to garnish

Slice cucumber lengthways into wide strips. Mix soured cream, mayonnaise, lemon juice and dried basil together. Lay salmon out flat into four sets of crosses. Spoon mayonnaise mixture into middle of each square. Fold up edges and wrap the two cucumber strips in a criss-cross over each parcel. Tuck end in underneath.

Garnish with lemon wedges.

Vol Au Vents

6 frozen vol au vent cases
1 tablespoon soy sauce (15 ml)
100 ml soured cream (4 fl oz)
1 tablespoon chopped parsley (15 ml)
1 egg yolk beaten
56 g previously cooked ham diced (2 oz)
Pinch nutmeg

Mix soured cream, parsley, egg yolk and nutmeg in bowl. Cook on medium – 40% for 4 minutes or until thick and creamy. Stir twice during this time. Add chopped ham and cook for a further minute.

Place vol au vent cases on sheet of grease proof paper in microwave, brush soy sauce around the edges with a pastry brush. Microwave on high for 3 minutes.

Fill with cream filling and serve hot.

Smoked Salmon Balls

168 g smoked salmon slices (6 oz)
84 g garlic and herb flavoured cream cheese (3 oz)
4 tablespoons creme fraiche or double cream (60 ml)
1 teaspoon gelatine (5 ml)
Juice of 1 lemon

Line 4 ramekin dishes with a quarter of the smoked salmon slices – leave long enough to hang over the dishes. Place remaining salmon slices, cream cheese and creme fraiche or double cream in a food processor and blend until smooth. Sprinkle gelatine over the lemon juice in a small bowl. Allow to stand for 5 minutes. Stand bowl in pan of steaming – not boiling – water which you should heat in the microwave for 2 minutes, until the gelatine has dissolved. Stir occasionally. Add dissolved gelatine to salmon mixture in food processor and blend for a few seconds until well mixed. Spoon into moulds and fold overhanging salmon slices over top. Cover moulds with cling film and chill for 4 hours before serving. Serve with slices of lemon.

TROUT PATE

448 g smoked trout fillets skinned (1 lb)
112 g cream cheese (4 oz)
2 tablespoons milk (30 ml)
3 tablespoons chopped chives (45 ml)

Flake fish, remove bones. Liquidise with cream cheese, milk and seasoning until smooth. Stir in chives. Spoon into 6 ramekin dishes and chill until required.

Soups

Fish Soup

4 tablespoons olive oil (60 ml)
1 small onion finely chopped
1 clove garlic crushed or finely chopped
2 sticks celery finely chopped
2 tablespoons parsley (30 ml)
150 ml dry white wine (6 fl oz)
392 g tinned chopped tomatoes (14 oz)
600 ml fish stock (24 fl oz)
224 g smoked haddock (8 oz)
224 g prawns defrosted (8 oz)
2 tablespoons parmesan cheese grated (30 ml)

Heat oil in casserole dish for 1 minute, add onion, garlic and celery and cook for 3 minutes. Stir in parsley, wine, tomatoes and stock. Cover and cook for 5 minutes. Add haddock and cook for 4 minutes covered. Remove haddock from dish and flake. Remove all bones. Return to casserole dish and add prawns and microwave for a further 4 minutes. Again cover the dish.

Pour into individual bowls and sprinkle the top with the parmesan cheese.

Fish Chowder

448 g smoked haddock (1 lb)
2 cloves garlic crushed or finely chopped
1 onion finely chopped
3 potatoes peeled and cubed
1 large carrot sliced

1 stick celery sliced
2 teaspoons margarine (10 ml)
3 streaky rashers
1 fish or vegetable stock cube
600 ml water (24 fl oz)
Half teaspoon mixed herbs (2.5 ml)
Freshly ground black pepper
Juice and rind of one lemon
300 ml milk (12 fl oz)

Put fish in casserole dish, cover with cold water and microwave for 2 minutes. Discard water. Remove bones from fish, cut into chunks. Melt margarine in dish for 15 seconds and add chopped rasher and cook for 2 minutes. Add onions and garlic. Cook for 2 minutes. Add remaining vegetables and cook for 3 minutes. Melt stock cube in a little water, just enough to cover the cube and microwave for 1 minute. Add to casserole and add remaining water, herbs and seasoning. Replace lid on casserole dish and cook for 6 minutes. Add milk and fish and cook for a further 6 minutes. Stir every two minutes.

Minestrone Soup

1 tablespoon oil (15 ml)
1 courgette finely chopped
1 carrot finely sliced or grated
1 leek finely sliced
1 stick celery finely chopped
1 potato peeled and cubed
1 clove garlic crushed or finely chopped
2 vegetable stock cubes dissolved in 1 lt – 40 fl oz water

392 g tin chopped tomatoes (14 oz)
56 g elbow macaroni (2 oz)
1 tablespoon tomato puree (15 ml)
28 g grated parmesan cheese (1 oz)
392 g tin red kidney beans (14 oz)

Place all vegetables and oil in casserole dish, cover and microwave on high for 5 minutes. Add vegetable stock, tomatoes, kidney beans, macaroni and tomato puree. Cover and cook for 10 minutes, stir twice during this time.

Allow to stand for 5 minutes.

Serve sprinkled with parmesan cheese.

CHUNKY BEEF SOUP

448 g chuck steak (1 lb)
1 tablespoon vegetable oil (15 ml)
1 onion sliced
448 g carrots sliced (1 lb)
2 tablespoons paprika (30 ml)
56 g flour (2 oz)
1 tablespoon tomato puree (15 ml)
1 lt beef stock – 40 fl oz
448 g potatoes peeled and sliced (1 lb)
1 tablespoon fresh parsley (15 ml)
4 tablespoons sherry – optional (60 ml)

Remove any fat or sinew from beef and cut into cubes. Heat vegetable oil in casserole dish for 1 minute, add beef and microwave uncovered on high for 3 minutes, stir every minute.

Add onions and carrots and cook on high for a further

two minutes. Drain fat, stir in paprika, flour, tomato puree and sherry. Gradually add stock and potatoes. Cover and microwave on high for 10 minutes. Stir every 3 minutes. Allow to stand for 5 minutes before serving. This could also be used as a main course.

MIXED VEGETABLE SOUP

224 g onions finely chopped (8 oz)
224 g potatoes peeled and grated (8 oz)
224 g carrots shredded (8 oz)
224 g leeks finely sliced (8 oz)
3 sticks celery sliced
2 vegetable stock cubes dissolved in 1 lt – 40 fl oz water
Ground black pepper
28 g butter or margarine (1 oz)
28 g cornflour mixed with a little milk (1 oz)

Melt butter in casserole dish for 45 seconds. Add all vegetables. Cover and cook for 4 minutes. Add stock. Cover and cook for a further 8 minutes. Add cornflour which has been mixed with a little milk, stir well into vegetable mixture. Cover and cook for 4 minutes. Stop twice during this time to stir.

Chicken Noodle Soup

1 small chicken (1 kg/2 lbs 2 oz)
2 carrots sliced
1 onion finely chopped
2 sticks celery sliced
Bay leaf
1 lt water (40 fl oz)
28 g noodles – alternatively use broken spagetti (1 oz)
Chopped parsley

Place chicken in casserole dish with all ingredients, add water and cover. Microwave on high for 20 minutes. Remove chicken and add some to the soup. Remove fat by drawing a piece of kitchen paper across the surface. Use remaining chicken in one of the other recipes. Remove bay leaf before serving.

Oxtail Soup

448 g oxtail cut into chunks (1 lb)
28 g margarine (1 oz)
2 onions chopped
2 sticks celery sliced
1 carrot sliced
1 lt beef stock – 2 stock cubes dissolved (40 fl oz)
28 g flour (1 oz)
1 teaspoon lemon juice (5 ml)

Place margarine in large casserole dish and microwave on high for 30–45 seconds until melted. Add oxtail pieces and coat with melted margarine. Add the vegetables and also coat with melted margarine. Add stock. Cover casserole dish and microwave on high for 20 minutes. Remove oxtail from soup and scrape meat from the bone. Add the meat to the soup. Allow the soup to cool and remove any fat from the surface with kitchen paper. Blend flour with a little water and add to the soup. Cover and microwave on high for 4 minutes. Stir twice or three times during this cooking period.

Add lemon juice and stir well.

MUSHROOM SOUP

56 g butter or margarine (2 oz)
56 g flour (2 oz)
600 ml milk & water mixed (24 fl oz)
1 vegetable stock cube
56 g sliced mushrooms (2 oz)

Melt butter in casserole dish or large pyrex jug. Add mushrooms and cook for 2 minutes. Add in flour and mix to a roux. Melt stock cube in a little of the milk and water mixture in a cup by microwaving for 1 minute. Add to remaining milk and water. Gradually add to roux blending slowly. Cover and microwave on high for 4 minutes. Stir three times during this cooking period.

Main Courses

Savoury Turkey and Ham Pie

448 g pre-cooked turkey (1 lb)
448 g pre-cooked ham (1 lb)
1 onion finely chopped
168 g sliced mushrooms (6 oz)
28 g margarine (1 oz)
2 tablespoons cornflour (30 ml)
5 tablespoons mayonnaise (75 ml)
300 ml milk (12 fl oz)
1 kg mashed potatoes (2lbs 2 oz)

Chop turkey and ham. Melt margarine in casserole dish for 30 seconds, add onions and mushrooms and cook for 2 minutes. Cover the casserole dish with the lid. Blend cornflour with a little of the milk and add to the onions and mushrooms, add remaining milk and cook for 2 minutes. Add turkey, ham and half the mayonnaise. Microwave for 3 minutes. Stir once during this time. Mix the remaining mayonnaise through the mashed potatoes. Spread the potato topping over the turkey and ham mixture.

Sprinkle paprika on top and microwave for 8 minutes. Do not cover.

Stand for 5 minutes before serving.

Turkey Cobbler

448 g pre-cooked turkey (1 lb)
2 tablespoons oil (30 ml)
1 large onion chopped
28 g flour (1 oz)
392 g tin tomatoes (14 oz)
1 teaspoon tobasco sauce (5 ml)
1 can sweetcorn

Scone topping
196 g self-raising flour (7 oz)
56 g margarine (2 oz)
1 teaspoon mixed herbs (5 ml)
150 ml soured cream (6 fl oz)

Place oil in casserole dish, add onion and cook for 2 minutes. Add turkey, mix in flour, then add the tomatoes, tobasco and seasoning. Microwave for 8 minutes stirring every 2 minutes.

To make scones
Rub margarine into flour until it resembles fine bread-crumbs. Stir in herbs and sour cream until it mixes together. Roll out and cut into 12 scone shapes.

Stir the sweet corn into the turkey mixture, place the scones on top in a circle and microwave uncovered for 6-8 minutes until scones are cooked.

TURKEY AND HAM LOAF

336 g pre-cooked turkey (12 oz)
224 g pre-cooked ham (8 oz)
1 small onion finely chopped
1 clove garlic finely chopped or crushed
1 teaspoon mixed herbs (5 ml)
1 large egg beaten
112 g fresh breadcrumbs (4 oz)
Half vegetable stock cube dissolved in 150 ml (6 fl oz)
Ground black pepper

Mince turkey, ham and onion in food processor. Add herbs, garlic, pepper, beaten egg, breadcrumbs and stock. Blend all together and press into a greased ring mould. If you do not have a ring mould you could use a large dish and put a glass half filled with water in the centre. Pack mixture around the dish and microwave on high for 8 minutes.

STEAKS IN GUINNESS

4 sirloin steaks

Marinade
3 teaspoons whole grain mustard (15 ml)
$^1/_2$ teaspoon ground cloves (2.5 ml)
$^1/_2$ teaspoon cinnamon (2.5 ml)
1 tablespoon soft brown sugar (15 ml)
8 peppercorns lightly crushed

300 ml Guinness (12 fl oz)
1 onion sliced
1 bay leaf

Mix mustard, spices, brown sugar and peppercorns together. Gradually add Guinness. Place steaks in shallow dish with onion slices and bay leaf. Stir marinade and pour over steaks. Leave in refrigerator for about 2–3 hours turning steaks occasionally. Arrange steaks on dish and microwave on high for 5 minutes.

Turkey and Broccoli Casserole

42 g butter (1½ oz)
3 tablespoons flour (45 ml)
½ vegetable stock cube
½ teaspoon dry mustard (2.5 ml)
300 ml milk (12 fl oz)
3 tablespoons mayonnaise (45 ml)
1 teaspoon lemon juice (5 ml)
224 g broccoli florets (8 oz)
448 g pre-cooked turkey (1 lb)
2 tablespoons grated parmesan cheese or white cheddar (30 ml)

Put butter in pyrex jug, microwave on high for 30 seconds to melt.

Beat in flour and mix to a roux, add crumbled vegetable stock cube and mustard. Gradually add milk and microwave on high for 2–3 minutes. Stop every minute and stir. Add mayonnaise and lemon juice. Put broccoli in casserole dish, cover and microwave for 4 minutes. Arrange turkey over broccoli, pour sauce over and microwave on high for 6 minutes. When cooked sprinkle cheese on top and the heat from underneath will melt same.

Turkey Bourguignon

2 streaky rashers
3 tablespoons butter (45 ml)
3 scallions thinly sliced
1 clove garlic finely chopped
224 g sliced mushrooms ($\frac{1}{2}$ lb)
2 tablespoons flour (30 ml)
150 ml red wine (6 fl oz)
$\frac{1}{2}$ beef stock cube dissolved in 150 ml water (6 fl oz)
2 tablespoons brandy (30 ml)
2 teaspoons Worcestershire sauce (10 ml)
$\frac{1}{2}$ teaspoon dried thyme (2.5 ml)
$\frac{1}{2}$ teaspoon ground black pepper (2.5 ml)
672 g pre-cooked turkey cut into cubes ($1\frac{1}{2}$ lbs)
336 g cooked rice or noodles (12 oz)

Place rashers on double thickness of kitchen paper and microwave for 1–2 minutes until rashers are brown and crisp. Crumble when cool. Put 2 tablespoons butter in casserole dish and melt for 45 seconds. Stir in scallions, garlic and crumbled rashers. Microwave for 1 minute. Add mushrooms and microwave for 3 minutes. Remove rashers and vegetables from casserole dish and set aside. Add remaining butter to casserole and microwave for 45 seconds. Stir in flour, blend in wine, stock, brandy, Worcestershire sauce, thyme and pepper. Microwave on high for 3–5 minutes until sauce is thick. Stir twice during this cooking time.

Stir turkey into sauce, cover and microwave for 4 minutes until turkey is hot. Stir in rashers and vegetables. Microwave again on high for a further 3 minutes. Serve with rice or noodles.

Turkey Stuffed with Apple

336 g self raising flour (12 oz)
168 g suet (6 oz)
Ground black pepper
1 medium sized cooking apple
4 thick slices cooked turkey
28 g chopped walnuts (1 oz)
1 tablespoon sage (15 ml)
2 tablespoons Worcestershire sauce (30 ml)

Sieve flour into bowl, add suet and seasonings, stir in sufficient cold water to bind to a fairly firm – not sticky – dough. Divide into 4 and roll each into a 20 cm/8 inch circle. Peel, core and thinly slice the apple. Place slices of turkey on each ring of pastry, top with apple slices, nuts and sage. Brush pastry edges with Worcestershire sauce. Fold pastry and pinch edges together. Brush outside with Worcestershire sauce. Cook on high for 8 minutes.

Duck à L'Orange

4 168 g duck breasts (6 oz)
2 tablespoons clear honey (30 ml)
1 tablespoon red wine vinegar (15 ml)
2 tablespoons port (30 ml)
Juice and rind of 1 orange
1 tablespoon redcurrant jelly (15 ml)
1 tablespoon cornflour (15 ml)

Place duck breasts on dish and brush with honey. Microwave on high for 4 minutes. Stop once to baste with juice and honey. Put red wine vinegar, port, orange juice, rind and redcurrant jelly in pyrex jug. Microwave on high for 5 minutes. Place duck on serving plates. Pour duck juices into sauce. Mix cornflour with a little water and add to sauce. Microwave on high for 2 minutes, stir every minute. Pour over duck and serve.

Duck with Port and Plum Sauce

4 leg portions duckling
Ground black pepper
112 g plum jam (4 oz)
200 ml apple juice (8 fl oz)
3 tablespoons port (45 ml)
$\frac{1}{2}$ teaspoon cornflour (2.5 ml)
1 tablespoon water (15 ml)

Prick duck portions all over at regular intervals with a fine skewer. Place on rack and microwave for 4 minutes. Microwave jam, apple juice and port for 2 minutes. Blend cornflour with water and stir into sauce. Microwave for 2 minutes, stop twice during this time to stir. Pour juices from duck into sauce and mix well. Place duck in casserole dish and pour sauce over. Cook for three minutes.

Guinness and Beef Stew

1 potato peeled and cubed
1 stick celery sliced
56 g flour (2 oz)
$^1/_2$ teaspoon nutmeg (2.5 ml)
448 g steak cut into cubes (1 lb)
3 tablespoons oil (45 ml)
28 g butter (1 oz)
2 onions finely chopped
2 cloves garlic crushed or finely chopped
1 teaspoon brown sugar (5 ml)
600 ml Guinness (24 fl oz)
Black pepper
1 teaspoon mixed herbs
2 carrots sliced

Sieve flour and nutmeg into bowl, coat meat with same. Microwave half the oil in a casserole dish for 2 minutes, add flour coated meat and cook for 6 minutes. Transfer meat to plate. Add remaining oil and butter to casserole dish. Add onion and garlic. Microwave for 3 minutes. Add brown sugar and cook for 1 minute to dissolve sugar. Add beef, Guinness, herbs, carrots, celery and potato to casserole. Microwave for 5 minutes. Add a little water if too thick. Cover and cook for 5 minutes. Allow to stand for 5 minutes.

Chicken and Mushroom Casserole

2 teaspoons margarine or butter (10 ml)
750 g chicken pieces (1 lb 12 oz)
600 ml mushroom soup (24 fl oz) see page 42

Melt margarine in casserole dish for 45 seconds, add chicken pieces and coat with butter. Cover with lid and microwave on high for 15 minutes. Pour soup over chicken pieces, cover and microwave for a further 6 minutes. Stir every 2 minutes.

Turkey and Ham Quiche

Pastry
168 g plain flour (6 oz)
$^{1}/_{2}$ teaspoon salt (2.5 ml)
56 g butter or margarine (2 oz)
28 g lard or white vegetable fat (1 oz)
2–3 tablespoons cold water combined with 3 drops yellow food colouring – optional (30–45 ml)

Sift together flour, salt and cut in butter and lard until the mixture resembles fine breadcrumbs. Add water and food colouring a little at a time, stirring with a fork until the mixture clings together. Form a ball and roll on a floured surface until it is 5 cm/2 inches larger than the top of a 24 cm/9 inch flan dish. Transfer to a dish and leave to settle in a refrigerator for 10 minutes. Trim around edge and prick pastry case with a fork all around the base and sides. Line the base with a double layer of kitchen paper. Microwave on high for 3 minutes. Remove paper.

Filling
$^{1}/_{2}$ red pepper deseeded and chopped
$^{1}/_{2}$ green pepper deseeded and chopped
1 onion finely chopped
6 mushrooms sliced
448 g previously cooked turkey and ham cut into cubes (1 lb)
1 teaspoon oil (5 ml)
112 g cheddar cheese grated (4 oz)
4 eggs
150 ml milk (6 fl oz)
Salt and pepper
Pinch of oregano

Place chopped peppers, onion, mushroom and oil in a bowl. Cover and microwave on high for 2 minutes. Beat eggs, milk and seasoning in a 1.2 litre/2 pint casserole dish. Microwave at medium – 50% for 5–8 minutes stirring every 2 minutes.

Add turkey and ham to pepper mixture and heat for 2 minutes.

Arrange the onions, peppers, mushrooms, turkey and

ham in the pastry case. Spread with grated cheese and pour the egg mixture over. Microwave on medium – 50% for 20 minutes. Sprinkle with grated cheese before serving.

Hot Turkey and Ham Curry

224 g previously cooked turkey (8 oz)
224 g previously cooked ham (8 oz)
1 onion finely chopped
1 level teaspoon cayenne pepper (5 ml)
1 level teaspoon turmeric (5 ml)
28 g butter or margarine (1 oz)
28 g flour (1 oz)
300 ml milk (12 fl oz)
3 teaspoons hot curry powder (15 ml)

In a pyrex jug melt the butter or margarine for 45 seconds. Add onions, curry powder, cayenne pepper and turmeric. Microwave on high for 2 minutes. Add flour and mix to a roux. Gradually add the milk blending well. Place turkey and ham on base of large casserole dish. Pour sauce over, cover and microwave on high for 4 minutes until the turkey and ham is warm. Stir twice during this time.

Ham and Pineapple Platter

4 thick slices previously cooked ham
4 pineapple rings from a tin of unsweetened pineapple

2 teaspoons cornflour (10 ml)

Place ham on large plate with pineapple ring on top of each slice of ham. Cover with lid of casserole dish and microwave on high for 4 minutes.

Pineapple Sauce
Blend cornflour with the pineapple juice from the tin of pineapples. Blend gradually. Microwave on high for 2 minutes. Stop twice during this time to stir.

Pour over the ham or serve in a sauce boat.

TURKEY AND HAM OMELETTE

4 eggs
4 tablespoons milk (60 ml)
Salt & pepper
Knob of butter
224 g previously cooked turkey and ham cut into cubes (8 oz)
1 onion finely chopped

Melt butter for 30 seconds, add onion and microwave on high for 2 minutes. Beat eggs and milk together. Pour egg mixture into greased pyrex casserole dish. Cook uncovered for 3–4 minutes. Place turkey, ham and onion over egg mixture. Cook for a further 2–3 minutes. When cooked, lift all around with spatula and flip over one half. Serve immediately

Turkey á la King

448 g previously cooked turkey (1 lb)
1 onion finely sliced
1 red pepper deseeded and sliced
1 green pepper deseeded and sliced
28 g sliced mushrooms (1 oz)
28 g butter or margarine (1 oz)
28 g flour (1 oz)
300 ml milk (12 fl oz)

Melt butter or margarine in large casserole dish for 45 seconds. Add mushrooms, peppers and onions. Microwave on high for 2 minutes. Add flour and mix to roux. Gradually add milk blending well. Microwave for 3 minutes, stirring every minute. Add chopped cold turkey and microwave for 2 minutes. Serve with rice.

Spiced Beef

672 g spiced beef (1½ lbs)
1 lt cold water (40 fl oz)

In large casserole dish place spiced beef, cover with cold water and replace lid on dish. Microwave on high for 20 minutes. Allow the meat to stand in the water until the meat cools down, preferably overnight. By leaving the meat cool in the water the flavour of the herbs and spices is stronger.

CHRISTMAS HAM

2 kg ham (4.4 lbs)
1 tablespoon honey (15 ml)
84 g demerara sugar mixed with 1 teaspoon dry mustard (3 oz)
Whole cloves

Put drained ham into a roasting bag, spread the honey on the skin of the ham. Arrange on an upturned saucer in a round casserole dish. Slit the roasting bag at the base to enable the steam to escape and microwave on high for 10 minutes. Turn the joint over and microwave on power 8 for a further 25 minutes. Allow to stand, covered with tin foil for 20 minutes.

Remove the ham and peel away the skin. Score the fat into diamond shapes with a sharp knife and press the sugar and mustard mixture into the fat. Press a clove into each diamond. Place under a pre-heated hot grill until the ham is crisp and brown. If preferred, you could remove the skin and coat the ham with toasted breadcrumbs instead of the sweet mixture.

TURKEY PLAIT

336 g plain flour (12 oz)
168 g butter or margarine (6 oz)
336 g previously cooked turkey (12 oz)
$\frac{1}{2}$ teaspoon salt (2.5 ml)
1 cooking apple peeled and sliced
Cold water

Salt and pepper
84 g breadcrumbs (3 oz)
14 g margarine ($\frac{1}{2}$ oz)
1 teaspoon mixed herbs (5 ml)
$\frac{1}{2}$ onion finely chopped
2 tablespoons Worcestershire sauce (30 ml)
1 tablespoon whole grain mustard (15 ml)
1 egg beaten
1 tablespoon milk (15 ml)
2 tablespoons poppy and sesame seeds (30 ml)

To Make Stuffing
Melt 14 g/$\frac{1}{2}$ oz butter for 30 seconds, add half onion and cook for 1 minute. Add to breadcrumbs and mixed herbs. Set aside.

To make pastry
Sieve flour and salt into bowl, rub in 168 g/6 oz margarine. Stir in 6 tablespoons/90 ml cold water, mix to soft dough. Place in refrigerator for 10 minutes. Mix the following together in a bowl. Cooked turkey, apple, whole grain mustard, beaten egg – reserve a little – Worcestershire sauce, salt and pepper.

Add stuffing mixture to turkey mixture. Roll pastry out in rectangular shape. Place all stuffing in centre of rectangle from top to end of rectangle. Cut strips of pastry from stuffing to the edge – Christmas tree shape. Dampen strips with water, bring up over filling taking one from each side to shape plait. Place in microwave, brush with milk and remaining egg. Sprinkle with seeds, microwave on high for 10 minutes.

Sweet and Sour Ham

448 g cooked ham cut into cubes (1 lb)
1 jar sweet and sour sauce or see page 84

In a large casserole dish microwave the cubed ham for 3 minutes.

Add the jar of sweet and sour sauce, cover and microwave for 4 minutes. Serve with rice.

Turkey and Ham in Red Wine

2 teaspoons oil (10 ml)
672 g previously cooked turkey and ham cubed (1½ lbs)
2 onions finely sliced
168 g mushrooms sliced (6 oz)
1 clove garlic crushed
1 vegetable stock cube dissolved in 300 ml water (12 fl oz)
150 ml red wine (6 fl oz)
1 teaspoon Worcestershire sauce (5 ml)
Freshly ground black pepper

Place oil, mushrooms, onions and garlic in casserole dish. Microwave on high for 3 minutes, stir twice during this time. Add stock, wine and Worcestershire sauce and microwave on high for 6 minutes – cover dish. Stir every 2 minutes. Add turkey and ham, cover and microwave on high for a further 4 minutes.

Turkey and Ham Cobbler

448 g previously cooked turkey (1 lb)
448 g previously cooked ham (1 lb)
Paprika
448 g previously cooked, mashed potatoes (1 lb)

Onion sauce
1 large onion sliced
28 g butter or margarine (1 oz)
28 g flour (1 oz)
$^1/_2$ clove garlic crushed or finely chopped
300 ml milk (12 fl oz)

Make up onion sauce
Melt butter in pyrex jug in microwave for 45 seconds, add
onion and garlic. Microwave for 2 minutes. Add flour and
mix to roux. Gradually add milk. Microwave on high for 2
minutes. Stop once during this time to stir.

Place turkey and ham on base of casserole dish, pour
onion sauce over and top with mashed potato. Sprinkle top
with paprika. Microwave on high for 8 minutes.

Stuffed Beef Rolls

56 g rindless streaky rashers (2 oz)
56 g butter (2 oz)
1 onion finely chopped
84 g white or brown breadcrumbs (3 oz)

28 g chopped walnuts (1 oz)
1 tablespoon dried parsley (15 ml)
672 g topside of beef (1½ lbs)
56 g flour (2 oz)
2 teaspoons tomato puree (10 ml)
150 ml red wine (6 fl oz)
450 ml water with 1 beef stock cube dissolved (18 fl oz)

Chop rashers finely. Melt 28 g/1 oz butter in pyrex jug for 45 seconds. Add rashers and onion. Cook for 2 minutes. Add breadcrumbs, parsley and walnuts, mix well and leave to cool.

Cut beef into 1.3 cm/½ inch – slices and flatten out to 0.5 cm/¼ inch thickness. Divide stuffing into each beef slice, roll up and secure with cocktail sticks or string. Melt remaining butter in casserole dish for 1 minute, add beef rolls. Microwave on high for 2 minutes. Remove beef, add flour to dish and mix to roux. Stir in puree, wine and stock. Microwave on high for 3 minutes. Stop once during cooking time to stir. Return beef to casserole, cover and cook for 10 minutes. Put beef rolls on plates and pour sauce over them.

TURKEY AND HAM IN PASTRY

1 pkt frozen puff pastry (224 g/8 oz)
4 thick slices of turkey
4 thick slices of ham
1 tablespoon soy sauce (15 ml)
300 ml cheese sauce (12 fl oz)

To make cheese sauce
28 g flour (1 oz)
28 g margarine (1 oz)
28 g grated cheddar cheese (1 oz)
300 ml milk (12 fl oz)

In pyrex jug, melt the butter for 45 seconds. Add flour and mix to a roux. Gradually blend in milk. Microwave on high for 2 minutes. Stir twice during this time. Fold the cheese into the sauce.

Roll out pastry and cut into four squares. Place one slice of ham on top of each slice of pastry, place slices of turkey on top of ham and pour tablespoon of cheese sauce over. Brush edges of pastry with soy sauce. Press edges down firmly. Brush pastry on top with soy sauce. Place in dish and microwave on high for 8 minutes.

Do not cover.

Main Course Potato Dish

1.5 kg potatoes (3$\frac{1}{2}$ lbs)
200 ml milk (8 fl oz)
300 ml cream (12 fl oz)
2 eggs
112 g grated cheddar cheese (4 oz)
2 cloves garlic
56 g butter (2 oz)
3 pinches nutmeg
Salt and pepper

Peel and clean potatoes, cut into 5 mm/$\frac{1}{4}$ inch slices, sprinkle generously with mix of nutmeg, salt and pepper. Mix well. Rub inside of dish with peeled clove of garlic, butter inside of dish. In bowl, mix together milk, cream and eggs. Add second clove of garlic crushed or finely chopped. Also add salt and pepper. Layer potatoes on base of casserole dish. Add grated cheese between layers until all potatoes are used. Pour mixture of milk, cream and eggs over potatoes. Finish with layer of cheese. Cook on high for 15 minutes. Stand for 5 minutes.

Turkey Stir Fry

4 tablespoons soy sauce (60 ml)
2 tablespoons vegetable oil (30 ml)
1 tablespoon sherry (15 ml)
224 g previously cooked turkey (8 oz)
1 green pepper deseeded and cut into strips
28 g sliced almonds (1 oz)
1 onion thinly sliced and separated into rings.

Combine soy sauce, oil and sherry in a bowl. Place turkey in marinade and allow to stand for 15–30 minutes. Place casserole dish containing turkey and all the other ingredients in microwave and cook on high for 8 minutes.

Serve with rice or noodles.

Turkey and Courgette Chinese Style

448 g previously cooked turkey (1 lb)
448 g courgettes (1 lb)
1 red pepper deseeded and thinly sliced
1 green pepper deseeded and thinly sliced
3 tablespoons vegetable oil (45 ml)
3 tablespoons sherry (45 ml)
1 tablespoon soy sauce (15 ml)
4 tablespoons natural yoghurt (60 ml)

Cut all ingredients into thin strips. Place courgettes, peppers, vegetable oil, sherry and soy sauce in casserole dish. Season lightly with salt and freshly ground black pepper. Cover and microwave on high for 4 minutes. Add sliced turkey and microwave for a further 4 minutes. Add yoghurt and stir just prior to serving.

Moussaka

448 g aubergines peeled and thinly sliced (1 lb)
5 tablespoons oil (75 ml)
448 g minced beef (1 lb)
56 g mushrooms chopped (2 oz)
1 large onion sliced
1 clove garlic crushed or finely chopped
420 g can chopped tomatoes (15 oz)

3 tablespoons tomato puree (45 ml)
1 teaspoon mixed herbs (5 ml)
Salt and pepper

Topping
2 eggs
150 ml cream (6 fl oz)
84 g grated cheddar cheese (3 oz)
1 tablespoon cornflour mixed with a little milk (15 ml)

Place oil in large casserole dish and microwave on high for 1 minute. Add sliced aubergine, cover and microwave on high for 2 minutes. Remove from dish and drain. Place the minced beef in the casserole dish and microwave on high for 2 minutes. Add onion, mushrooms and garlic and microwave on high for a further 3 minutes. Add tomato puree, chopped tomatoes, mixed herbs, salt and pepper. Stir in cornflour and mix well. Grease a dish suitable for microwave use, layer with ladle of mince, then layer with slices of aubergine, continue to layer but finish with layer of aubergine. Cover and microwave on high for 3 minutes. In a separate bowl mix together the topping ingredients.

Pour sauce over moussaka. Microwave on half power – 50% for 5 minutes. Do not cover. Allow to stand for 5 minutes before serving.

You can brown the topping under a pre-heated grill if desired.

FISH DISHES

Smoked Salmon in Pastry

224 g frozen puff pastry defrosted (8 oz)
1 egg beaten
224 g smoked salmon (8 oz)
4 tablespoons dry white wine
168 g button mushrooms sliced (6 oz)
14 g butter or margarine ($^1/_2$ oz)
$^1/_2$ tablespoon cornflour (7.5 ml)
300 ml milk (12 fl oz)
2 tablespoons fresh dill (30 ml)

Roll out pastry, cut into four squares. Brush with beaten egg, score with sharp knife. Place on grease proof paper and microwave for 5 minutes. Trim the fish and cut into bite sized squares. Sprinkle half of the wine over and microwave for 4 minutes. Melt butter in casserole dish, add mushrooms and cook for 2 minutes. Mix together remaining wine and cornflour. Add milk to mushrooms, cook for 2 minutes, stir in wine mixture. Cook for 1 minute and stir. Add salmon and dill. Spoon salmon and sauce onto a plate and top with slice of pastry.

Fish Kebabs

8 wooden skewers
448 g cod (1 lb)
1 red pepper deseeded
1 green pepper deseeded
8 cherry tomatoes
8 button mushrooms
Jar of pickled onions

Marinade
1 finely chopped onion
4 tablespoons olive oil (60 ml)
4 tablespoons lemon juice (60 ml)
1 teaspoon mixed herbs

Add peppers, tomatoes, mushrooms and fish to marinade. Cover and allow to stand for at least 2 hours. Thread cod and peppers, cut into chunks, tomatoes, mushrooms and pickled onions on a skewer. Place on a plate or lid of casserole dish, brush with marinade and cook the 8 kebabs on high for 4 minutes.

Whiting Rounds

6 strips of whiting
6 cherry tomatoes
Cocktail sticks

Wrap strips of whiting around tomato and secure with cocktail sticks. Place in circle on a plate and cook for 3 minutes.

Curried Smoked Haddock

448 g smoked haddock (1 lb)
1 finely chopped onion
600 ml cold water (24 fl oz)
28 g butter (1 oz)
28 g flour (1 oz)
2 teaspoons curry powder (10 ml)
300 ml milk (12 fl oz)

Place fish in casserole dish and cover with cold water. Cover and microwave on high for 2 minutes. Discard water. In pyrex jug melt butter for 45 seconds, add onion and curry powder and microwave for 2 minutes. Add flour and mix to a roux. Gradually add milk, and cook for 2 minutes. Stop and stir twice. Pour over fish and microwave on high for 3 minutes.

Brill in Cider Sauce

448 g brill skinned and cut into chunks (1 lb)
42 g flour (1½ oz)
70 g butter (2½ oz)
1 onion finely chopped
Chopped parsley

Cider Sauce
300 ml dry cider (12 fl oz)
28 g butter (1 oz)
1 tablespoon lemon juice
28 g flour (1 oz)

Coat fish with flour, melt butter, add onion and cook for 2 minutes. Remove onion and fish to another dish. Make sauce – add butter to remaining butter in dish. Melt by microwaving for 45 seconds. Stir in flour. Gradually add cider and lemon juice. Cook for 2 minutes. Pour over fish and cook for 4 minutes. Garnish with chopped parsley.

Whiting in Pineapple Sauce

448 g whiting (1 lb)
Pineapple sauce (see page 56)
Pineapple rings to decorate

Place whiting in casserole dish, cover and microwave on high for 5 minutes. Use juices from fish to add to pineapple sauce. Pour sauce over whiting when serving. Decorate with sliced pineapples.

Cod in Wine Sauce

56 g mushrooms sliced (2 oz)
336 g cod cut into cubes (12 oz)
56 g prawns defrosted (2 oz)
1 tomato sliced

Wine Sauce
28 g butter or margarine (1 oz)
28 g flour (1 oz)
Salt and pepper
150 ml white wine (6 fl oz)
150 ml water with vegetable stock cube dissolved (6 fl oz)

Sauce: place butter in 1 litre/40 fl oz jug and microwave on high for 1 minute. Stir in flour, salt and pepper and mix to roux. Gradually add the wine and stock stirring continuously. Microwave on high for 2–3 minutes. Stir in the mushrooms, cubed fish and prawns.

Place in large casserole dish, cover and microwave on high for 6 minutes. Garnish with tomato slices.

Vegetables

Baked Cabbage

896 g cabbage chopped (2 lbs)
150 ml mushroom soup (6 fl oz) – see p. 42
½ teaspoon salt (2.5 ml)
56 g butter (2 oz)
150 ml milk (6 fl oz)
1 onion finely chopped
56 g flour (2 oz)

Place cabbage, soup and salt in casserole dish, cover and microwave on high for 12 minutes. Add butter, milk and onion. Cover and microwave for 3 minutes. Stir in flour. Microwave again for 3 minutes – stop and stir every minute at this stage.

Creamy Mushrooms

12 large mushrooms sliced
1 clove garlic finely chopped
3 tablespoons parlsey (45 ml)
28 g grated cheese (1 oz)
28 g butter (1 oz)
1 tablespoon flour (15 ml)
Salt and pepper
1 onion finely chopped
150 ml cream (6 fl oz)

Melt 28 g (1 oz) butter in casserole dish for 45 seconds. Add mushrooms, onion and garlic. Cover and cook for 3 minutes.

77

Add flour and blend well. Add cream and cook for $1\frac{1}{2}$ minutes until the mixture thickens. Stir in the parsley and seasonings. Serve with grated cheese.

JULIENNE CARROTS

2 carrots
1 tablespoon lemon juice (15 ml)

Cut a carrot into chunks and divide in two lengthways. Then slice lengthways, cut into two and create matchstick-like strips. Continue with the remaining carrot. Place in pyrex jug, pour lemon juice over, and cover jug with a saucer. Microwave for $4\frac{1}{2}$ minutes.

ONIONS WITH CHEESE

4 onions sliced in rings
56 g cheddar cheese cut into cubes (2 oz)
2 teaspoons sugar (10 ml)
1 teaspoon lemon juice (5 ml)
Parsley to garnish

Place onions, lemon juice, sugar and half the cheese in casserole dish. Cover and microwave for 3 minutes. Stir every minute. Add remaining cheese and microwave again for 3 minutes. Sprinkle with parlsey and serve.

Lemon Brussel Sprouts

448 g fresh brussel sprouts (1 lb)
2 tablespoons water (30 ml)
28 g butter (1 oz)
2 tablespoons lemon juice (30 ml)
Grated rind of 1 lemon
Pinch of garlic powder

Discard loose leaves of brussel sprouts. Cut a shallow cross on base of each sprout. Place sprouts and water in casserole dish, cover and microwave on high for 8 minutes. Allow to stand for 3 minutes. Melt butter in a small bowl for 30 seconds. Add lemon juice, grated rind and garlic powder. Drain sprouts, add butter mixture and coat.

Marinated Vegetables

224 g broccoli florets (8 oz)
224 g cauliflower florets (8 oz)
1 large carrot, thinly sliced
2 tablespoons water (30 ml)
224 g button mushrooms (8 oz)
4 cherry tomatoes halved

Marinade:
100 ml white wine vinegar (4 fl oz)
1 clove garlic crushed

1 small onion finely chopped
3 tablespoons extra olive oil (45 ml)
1$\frac{1}{2}$ teaspoons brown sugar (7.5 ml)
$\frac{1}{2}$ teaspoon dried oregano (2.5 ml)
$\frac{1}{2}$ teaspoon mustard powder (2.5 ml)

To prepare marinade: Place wine vinegar, garlic and onion in dish and microwave for 30 seconds. Allow to stand for 1 hour. Add all other ingredients.

In large casserole combine broccoli, cauliflower and carrots, add water, cover and microwave for 8 minutes. Drain, add mushrooms and tomatoes. Pour marinade over vegetables. Cover and refrigerate for 3–4 hours.

SAUCES

Hollandaise Sauce

3 egg yolks
2 tablespoons lemon juice (30 ml)
Salt and pepper
84 g butter (3 oz)

Blend egg yolks and lemon juice and beat until frothy. Heat butter in pyrex jug for 1 minute. Blend egg yolks with butter and microwave on low for 3 minutes. Stop and stir twice during cooking.

Barbecue Sauce

1 tablespoon oil (15 ml)
1 onion finely chopped
1 clove garlic finely chopped or crushed
150 ml water (6 fl oz)
2 tablespoons vinegar (30 ml)
2 tablespoon brown sugar (30 ml)
2 teaspoons mustard (10 ml)
1 slice lemon
Pinch dried thyme
Pinch cayenne pepper
2 tablespoons Worcestershire sauce (30 ml)
5 tablespoons tomato ketchup (75 ml)
2 tablespoons tomato puree (30 ml)
Freshly ground black pepper

Place oil, onion, garlic in pyrex jug or casserole dish and cook for 2 minutes. Stir in all ingredients and heat for 2 minutes. Remove lemon slice. Cook for 2 minutes.

Stir Fry Sauce

3 tablespoons soy sauce (45 ml)
3 tablespoons pineapple juice (45 ml)
1 onion finely chopped
1 tablespoon vegetable oil (15 ml)
1 tablespoon cornflour (15 ml)

Place oil in pyrex jug or casserole dish with the onion. Microwave on high for 2 minutes. Add soy sauce and pineapple juice and microwave for 1 minute. Blend cornflour with a little pineapple juice and add to sauce. Microwave on high for 2 minutes. Stop and stir twice during this time.

Sweet and Sour Sauce

56 g brown sugar (2 oz)
56 g vinegar (2 oz)
84 g pineapple chunks and juice, unsweetened (3 oz)
1–2 tablespoons soy sauce (15–30 ml)
2 tablespoons oil (30 ml)

1 clove of garlic chopped finely
28 g sliced mushrooms (1 oz)
2 tablespoons (30 ml) cornflour blended with ¹/₂ cup of water

Heat the oil in a casserole dish or a measuring jug for 2 minutes. Add the mushrooms and cook on high for 1 minute. Add all the other ingredients and cook on high for 5 minutes. Stir once during cooking.

The above sauce is ideal with chicken pieces, pork pieces or with beef. Also try with left over bacon.

Desserts

Tropical Pavlova

1 egg white
308 g icing sugar sifted (11 oz)
175 ml creme fraiche (7 fl oz)
14 g caster sugar ($\frac{1}{2}$ oz)
150 ml double cream lightly whipped (6 fl oz)
1 small tin pineapple drained and dried in kitchen paper
2 kiwi fruit peeled and cut into slices
2 mandarin oranges peeled and separated
14–16 grapes halved and deseeded

Lightly beat egg white, stir in icing sugar with metal spoon, knead to form firm fondant. Divide into 16 and roll into small balls when the mixture is like a dough. Arrange 8 in a circle on grease proof paper and lift into microwave. Cook for $1\frac{1}{2}$ –2 minutes until 4 times their size and they have merged together to form the pavalova base. Leave to cool in microwave. As the remaining 8 are to be individual meringues put 4 fondant balls in microwave on grease proof paper and cook for 1 minute. Leave to cool in microwave. Repeat with remaining mixture. Fold together creme fraiche, whipped cream and sugar. Put meringue base on to serving dish and spoon on two-thirds of the mixture. Pile pineapple, kiwi, orange segments and grapes on top. Spoon a little cream on base of each individual meringue and arrange on top of fruit. Scatter over remaining fruit. Serve within an hour.

Strawberry Mousse

1 tin strawberries (448 g/14 oz)
1 packet strawberry jelly
600 ml cream (24 fl oz)
4 egg whites
56 g caster sugar (2 oz)
1 tablespoon brandy (15 ml)

Melt jelly cube for 45 seconds in casserole dish, drain juice from strawberries and add juice to melted jelly. Whisk egg whites until stiff and fold into jelly mixture. Whip cream and divide into two bowls. To half amount of cream add caster sugar and rum. Fold into jelly. Hold back several strawberries for decoration. Crush remaining strawberries and fold into mousse when almost set. Decorate with remaining whipped cream and strawberries.

Mince Pies

224 g plain flour (8 oz)
56 g icing sugar (2 oz)
140 g margarine (5 oz)
Beat together the following:
1 egg yolk, cold water (15 ml) and $\frac{1}{2}$ teaspoon lemon juice (2.5 ml)

Filling
336 g mincemeat (12 oz). See recipe on pp. 91–2

Pastry

Place all ingredients [keeping a little egg] in bowl and mix well. Roll out two-thirds pastry on lightly floured board. Cut into rounds with cutter slightly larger than the spaces in baking tray. Line trays with these cut out rounds of pastry. Place rounds of kitchen paper over each and microwave for 2 minutes. Remove kitchen paper and fill with mincemeat. Cut rest of pastry into smaller rounds to fit on top. Brush around tops with water to seal. Mark two slits in centre of each. Lightly beat left over egg with fork and brush over pies and sprinkle with dark brown sugar. Microwave on 50% for 4 minutes.

Home-Made Mincemeat

1 large lemon
224 g cooking apples peeled and sliced (8 oz)
224 g currants (8 oz)
112 g raisins (4 oz)
112 g sultanas (4 oz)
112 g mixed peel (4 oz)
56 g cherries quartered (2 oz)
112 g brown sugar (4 oz)
$\frac{1}{2}$ level teaspoon mixed spice (2.5 ml)
$\frac{1}{2}$ level teaspoon ground nutmeg (2.5 ml)
$\frac{1}{2}$ level teaspoon cinnamon (2.5 ml)
$\frac{1}{4}$ teaspoon ground ginger (1.25 ml)
112 g shredded suet (4 oz)

4 tablespoons brandy, whiskey or rum (60 ml)

Sterilise two x 448 g (1 lb) and one 224 g (½ lb) jam jars. See *Hints and Tips* on sterilising jars.

Wash lemon and grate it finely. Cut in half and squeeze the juice. Place all fruit, sugar and spices in mixing bowl, add grated lemon rind and juice and mix well. Add shredded suet and spirits. Mix well. Fill the jars, cover and leave for at least two weeks before using.

Plum Pudding

84 g fresh breadcrumbs (3 oz)
84 g plain flour (3 oz)
Pinch nutmeg
Pinch cinnamon
84 g shredded suet (3 oz)
56 g soft brown sugar (2 oz)
56 g caster sugar (2 oz)
56 g candied peel (2 oz)
56 g currants (2 oz)
140 g raisins (5 oz)
140 g sultanas (5 oz)
42 g chopped almonds (1½ oz)
1 small cooking apple peeled and sliced
Grated rind and juice of 1 lemon
4 tablespoons brandy (60 ml)
1 large egg beaten

300 ml stout (12 fl oz)
2 tablespoons black treacle (30 ml)

In large mixing bowl mix breadcrumbs with flour, nutmeg, cinnamon, suet and sugars. In separate bowl mix peel, currants, raisins, sultanas, almonds and apple. Mix well. Blend lemon rind and juice with brandy, egg, stout and milk. Add to dry ingredients and add black treacle. Add fruit mixture and mix to a soft dripping consistency. Cover and leave to stand overnight or for 6-8 hours. Turn into grease proof paper lined or microwave cling film lined pudding bowls. This mixture makes 2 x 1.2 litres – 2 pt puddings. Cover loosely with sheet of microwave cling film. Cook each pudding on high for 8 minutes. Allow to stand for 5 minutes before turning out. These puddings can be made up to four weeks in advance. If, however, you wish to store these puddings for longer, freeze them. To reheat when required, microwave on high for 3 minutes and again allow to stand for 5 minutes to allow the pudding to heat through. Serve with either brandy butter or brandied cream.

Brandy Butter
112 g icing sugar (4 oz)
1 tablespoon spreadable butter (15 ml)
2 tablespoons brandy (30 ml)

Gradually add icing sugar to butter and mix in with a wooden spoon. Add brandy and mix well. Chill in refrigerator for 10 – 15 minutes before using.

Brandied Cream
300 ml cream (12 fl oz)
28 g icing sugar sifted (1 oz)
1 tablespoon brandy (15 ml)

Whip cream, fold icing sugar into cream, add brandy.
  Pour over plum pudding just before serving.

Rhubarb Crumble

672 g rhubarb washed and trimmed (1$\frac{1}{2}$ lbs)
84 g demerara sugar (3 oz)
168 g wholemeal flour (6 oz)
112 g butter or margarine (4 oz)
28 g walnuts finely chopped (1 oz)

Cut rhubarb into 2.5 cm/1 inch pieces and place in a casserole
dish. Add 28 g/1 oz demerara sugar and mix thoroughly. Cover
and microwave on high for 4–5 minutes until the rhubarb
softens. Stir twice during this time. Sift the flour into a mixing
bowl and rub in the butter until the mixture resembles fine
breadcrumbs. Stir in the remaining sugar and the walnuts.
Spoon the crumble mixture on top of the rhubarb. Microwave on
high for 10 minutes. Allow to stand for five minutes before
serving.

Sherry Trifle

1 block jelly
450 ml cold water (18 fl oz)
1 pkt trifle sponges
600 ml milk (24 fl oz)
3 tablespoons custard powder (45 ml)
2 tablespoons sugar (30 ml)
300 ml cream whipped (12 fl oz)
Grated chocolate

Place block of jelly in casserole dish, do not add water. Microwave on high for 45 seconds to dissolve jelly. Gradually add cold water stirring constantly. Place trifle sponges in jelly. Allow to stand in refrigerator for 1 hour. Place milk in pyrex jug and microwave for 2 minutes on high. Mix custard powder and sugar with a little milk and mix to a paste. Add to heated milk and stir well. Microwave on high for 2 minutes. Stir twice during this time. Stir for several minutes while cooling down. When cool pour over set trifle. Return to refrigerator to set. Before serving pour whipped cream on top and sprinkle with grated chocolate.

If preferred, before pouring whipped cream over trifle, add two tablespoons of icing sugar to whipped cream and 2 tablespoons sherry.

Swiss Pudding

1 orange or lemon Swiss roll
2 orange or lemon blocks of jelly
4 mandarin oranges
Water

Slice Swiss roll and line base and sides of pudding bowl.

Reserve enough to cover top of bowl when full. Peel mandarin oranges and break into segments. Place blocks of jelly in pyrex jug and microwave on high for 45 seconds to 1 minute to dissolve. Gradually fill to 900 ml/36 fl oz level with cold water, stirring continuously. Pour into pudding bowl over Swiss roll. Drop individual orange segments into jelly. Cover jelly with remaining slices of Swiss roll and stand in refrigerator overnight. If using tinned fruit, use juice from tin to add to dissolved jelly and top with cold water.

Seasonal Dessert

56 g butter (2 oz)
56 g dark brown sugar (2 oz)
1 teaspoon ground cinnamon (5 ml)
3 teaspoons rum or brandy or port (45 ml)
2 pears cut in half, seeds removed
2 kiwis peeled and sliced
112 g black grapes halved and seeded (4 oz)

In casserole dish place butter and sugar, cover and microwave for 2 minutes until butter has melted and sugar dissolved. Add cinnamon and alcohol. Stir well and microwave for a further two minutes. Add pears, kiwis and grapes, stir well. Cover and microwave for 2 minutes. Serve with fresh cream or ice cream.

Pear and Walnut Pudding

224 g butter or margarine (8 oz)
252 g demerara sugar (9 oz)
Grated rind of 1 lemon
3 eggs
168 g self-raising flour (6 oz)
1 tablespoon self-raising flour (15 ml)
$^1/_2$ teaspoon baking powder (2.5 ml)
2 firm pears
112 g chopped walnuts (4 oz)

Beat 56 g/2 oz butter with 84 g /3 oz sugar. Spread this over base of a deep microwave proof dish. Sprinkle 56 g/2 oz walnuts over the above. Cream remaining butter and sugar with grated rind of lemon. Beat in eggs. Sift flour and baking powder. Fold into mixture with remaining walnuts. Peel, core and dice pears, toss in 1 tablespoon/15 ml flour. Fold into mixture. Microwave on high for 8 minutes. Allow to cool before turning out.

Serve with whiskey/brandy cream – see page 94.

Tea Time
Treats

Irish Coffee Cake

168 g margarine (6 oz)
4 tablespoons instant coffee (60 ml) dissolved in 1 tablespoon
    boiling water and cooled (15 ml)
168 g caster sugar (6 oz)
3 eggs
168 g self-raising flour (6 oz)
200 ml strong black coffee (8 fl oz)
168 g sugar (6 oz)
7 tablespoons Irish whiskey (110 ml)

Decoration
300 ml cream (12 fl oz)
2 tablespoons icing sugar (30 ml)
Grated chocolate or chopped nuts

Place margarine, instant coffee, caster sugar, eggs and flour in bowl and beat until well mixed. Place in ring moulds or dish with half glass of water in the centre to form a ring mould. Microwave on high for 8 minutes.

Dissolve sugar in the strong black coffee and microwave on high for 2 minutes, add whiskey. Pour hot coffee syrup over cake. Allow to stand for 1–2 hours. Whip cream until stiff and add icing sugar, fold in 1 tablespoon of whiskey. Before serving, pour cream over cake and decorate with either the grated chocolate or chopped nuts.

Carrot Cake

168 g margarine (6 oz)
168 g dark brown sugar (6 oz)
2 tablespoons black treacle (30 ml)
3 eggs lightly whisked
224 g grated carrot (8 oz)
112 g chopped walnuts and almonds – half and half (4 oz)
168 g plain flour (6 oz)
$\frac{1}{2}$ teaspoon baking powder (2.5 ml)
$\frac{1}{2}$ teaspoon cinnamon (2.5 ml)
$\frac{1}{2}$ teaspoon nutmeg (2.5 ml)
28 g bran (1 oz)

Microwave margarine in casserole dish for 2 minutes to melt, and allow to cool for 2 minutes. Place sugar and black treacle in bowl and add melted margarine with lightly beaten eggs and mix well. Stir in grated carrots, chopped walnuts/almonds. Sieve the flour, baking powder and spices together then fold with the bran into the mixture. Pour mixture into large greased casserole dish – preferably line the base with grease proof paper to enable you to take out of the dish. Microwave for 13 minutes. Allow to cool before turning out.

Topping
224 g icing sugar (8 oz)
112 g cream cheese (4 oz)
56 g spreadable butter (2 oz)
1 teaspoon vanilla essence (5 ml)
1 teaspoon sherry (5 ml)

4 whole walnuts

Beat all the above ingredients together until fluffy. Spread over cake when cool. Decorate with walnuts.

KATIE'S PORTER CAKE

448 g plain flour (1 lb)
224 g dark brown sugar (½ lb)
224 g margarine (½ lb)
3 large eggs
½ teaspoon mixed spice (2.5 ml)
¼ teaspoon bread soda (1.25 ml)
300 ml stout (12 fl oz)
448 g sultanas (1 lb)
112 g halved cherries (4 oz)
112 g mixed peel (4 oz)
2 tablespoons black treacle (30 ml)

Place margarine, sugar and stout in large casserole dish and microwave on high for 3 minutes. Remove and stir constantly until margarine has dissolved. Add all fruit and black treacle except cherries. Allow to cool. Sieve flour [keeping one tablespoon aside], bread soda and spices in bowl. Beat eggs in separate bowl. Add flour to fruit mixture. Dust cherries lightly in flour to avoid sinking. Add cherries to mixture then stir in eggs. Line two casserole dishes with either cling film or grease proof paper and cook each cake on high for 10 minutes. Stand for 10 minutes before turning out.

No Bake Cake

140 g digestive biscuits (5 oz)
112 g glacé cherries halved (4 oz)
224 g dates chopped (8 oz)
196 g unsalted peanuts (7 oz)
196 g fruit and nut chocolate chopped (7 oz)
280 g plain chocolate chopped (10 oz)
2 tablespoons golden syrup or honey (30 ml)
56 g butter (2 oz)
84 g white chocolate (3 oz)

Crush biscuits with rolling pin, put in bowl with cherries, dates and peanuts. Mix well. Put syrup/honey, butter, fruit, nut and plain chocolate in casserole dish and microwave for 3–4 minutes until melted. Pour into biscuit mixture and mix well. Line flan dish with microwave cling film or grease proof paper. Spoon mixture into flan dish. Press down firmly and chill for 2 hours in refrigerator. Melt white chocolate in pyrex jug by microwaving for 2 minutes. Pour over cake to your own design. Chill for 15 minutes before removing from dish.

CHOCOLATE RICE CRISPIES

1 block cooking chocolate (168 g/6 oz)
Packet of rice crispies (42 g/1$\frac{1}{2}$ oz)
Paper cases

Place block of chocolate in casserole dish and microwave on high for 1$\frac{1}{2}$ minutes. Stop and stir after 1 minute. When melted stir in the rice crispies. While still warm spoon mixture into pastry cases.

As an alternative use either orange flavoured or mint flavoured chocolate.

CHEESE FONDUE

224 g cheddar cheese grated (8 oz)
224 g gruyere cheese grated (8 oz)
5 tablespoons cornflour (75 ml)
1 teaspoon dry mustard (5 ml)
2 teaspoons Worcestershire sauce (10 ml)
$\frac{1}{4}$ teaspoon nutmeg (1.25 ml)
$\frac{1}{4}$ teaspoon black pepper (1.25 ml)
1 clove garlic crushed
450 ml dry white wine (18 fl oz)
3 tablespoons dry sherry (45 ml)

Mix cheeses, nutmeg, mustard, Worcestershire sauce, pepper and garlic in large bowl. Set aside. Blend cornflour with half the wine. Pour remaining wine into casserole dish, heat on medium for 4 minutes until wine is hot. Stir in cheese mixture, microwave on medium for 3 minutes until cheese melts. Stir well. Stir in blended cornflour and cook on medium for 6 minutes, stir every 2 minutes. Stir in sherry. Serve with crusty French bread cut into small squares.

Macaroni Cheese

168 g macaroni (6 oz)
1 litre boiling water (40 fl oz)
56 g butter (2 oz)
56 g flour (2 oz)
600 ml milk (24 fl oz)
168 g cheddar cheese (6 oz)

Put macaroni and boiling water in casserole dish and cook on high for 10–12 minutes. Drain. Place butter in pyrex jug and melt by microwaving for 1 minute, stir in flour and mix to a roux. Gradually blend in milk until evenly mixed. Cook for 3 minutes, until thick. Add three quarters of the cheese, mix well and add to macaroni. Microwave for 3–4 minutes. Sprinkle remaining cheese over top. Serve at once.

Mother's Brown Bread

448 g wholemeal flour (1 lb)
112 g white flour (4 oz)
112 g bran (4 oz)
56 g porridge oatlets (2 oz)
1 teaspoon salt (5 ml)
1 teaspoon bread soda (5 ml)
1 litre buttermilk (40 fl oz)
1 egg
2 tablespoons oil (30 ml)

Mix all ingredients together – dry ingredients first, then slowly adding a little buttermilk with beaten egg, then add the oil and the rest of the buttermilk stirring all the time. Grease a casserole dish and pour mix into dish. Do not cover. Microwave on high for 20 minutes or use two dishes and microwave each loaf for 10 minutes.

Halloween Barm Brack

448 g sliced and peeled cooking apples (1 lb)
224 g butter or margarine (8 oz)
224 g brown sugar (8 oz)

112 g wholemeal flour (4 oz)
224 g plain white flour (8 oz)
1 teaspoon baking powder (5 ml)
2 teaspoons mixed spice (10 ml)
1 teaspoon cinnamon (5 ml)
1 teaspoon nutmeg (5 ml)
448 g mixed fruit – sultanas, raisins, currants, etc. (1 lb)
112 g chopped walnuts (4 oz)
2 tablespoons black treacle (15 ml)

Place apples and sugar in pyrex dish, microwave on high for 3 minutes, stir and make sure sugar has dissolved. If necessary microwave for another 1–2 minutes. Add butter and treacle, stir until dissolved. Allow to cool. Add flours, spices and baking powder to mixture. Add fruit and mix well. Divide mixture into two casserole dishes. Cook each brack for 10 minutes on high. Allow to stand for 10 minutes before turning out.

Whiskey Marmalade

672 g Seville oranges washed (1½ lbs)
Juice of 1 lemon
1.4 kg sugar (3 lb)
150 ml whiskey (6 fl oz)
1.7 litres water (3 pints)

Halve oranges. Squeeze out juice and pips. Wrap pips and membrane from oranges in muslin, tie securely. Slice orange peel into thick strips. Put into large casserole dish with orange and lemon juice, muslin bag and 1.7 lt/3 pints water. Microwave on high for 5 minutes. Do not cover. Remove muslin bag. Add sugar and stir until dissolved. Cook on 50% for 20 minutes. Stir in whiskey and allow to stand for 5 minutes. Prepare 5 x 448 /1 lb jars, see Hints and Tips for sterilising jars. Stir again before pouring into jars. Cover with waxed paper.

DRINKS

Lemonade

Juice and grated rind of 2 lemons
112 g castor sugar (4 oz)
2 tablespoons water (30 ml)

Combine the above in a pyrex jug and microwave on high for 2 minutes, stir twice during cooking time.

Cool mixture in the refrigerator until cold. To serve, dilute 50 ml/2 fl oz of lemonade with 300 ml – 12 fl oz of water.

Mulled Wine

1 standard bottle of red wine
$\frac{1}{3}$ bottle of water
1 cup orange juice
1 cup port
1 cup sugar
$\frac{1}{2}$ teaspoon ground cloves (2.5 ml)
2 cinnamon sticks
1 lemon sliced

Combine all the ingredients except the lemon slices. Microwave on high for 12–14 minutes. Do not allow the mixture to boil. Garnish with sliced lemon.

Irish Coffee

150 ml water (6 fl oz)
1 teaspoon sugar (5 ml)
1½ teaspoons instant coffee (7.5 ml)
2 teaspoons whipped cream (10 ml)
3 tablespoons Irish whiskey (45 ml)

Bring the water to the boil in the glass. Add the sugar and stir until melted. Add the instant coffee and stir well. Add the whiskey and stir. Add the whipped cream gradually by running the spoon along the rim of the glass. Decorate with a few coffee granules on top of the cream.

Irish Cream Liqueur

1 can condensed milk (392 g/14 oz)
1 can evaporated milk (420 g/ 15 oz)
1½ teaspoons glycerine (7.5 ml)
1½ teaspoons chocolate essence (7.5 ml)
1 cup whiskey

Mix all the above together and whip well.
    You do not require a microwave for this recipe but I just thought that you would be interested in it.

VARIABLE POWER CHART

100%	FULL	FULL	10
90%	FULL	REHEAT	9
80%	FULL	ROAST	8
70%	FULL	BAKE	7
60%	MEDIUM	MEDIUM	6
50%	MEDIUM	SIMMER	5
40%	MEDIUM	SIMMER	4
30%	LOW	DEFROST	3
20%	LOW	WARM	2
10%	LOW	LOW	1

Defrosting Chart

Type	Quantity	Method	Defrost time	Standing time
chicken drumsticks	4	place thin parts towards centre of dish	6 mins	5 mins
portions	2x224g/8 oz	turn over half-way	6 mins	5 mins
whole	per 448 g/1 lb	turn half-way	17 mins	10 mins
turkey whole	per 448 g/1 lb [max 4.5 kg/10 lb]	turn over and around 4 times while defrosting	6 mins	20 mins
duck	per 448 g/1 lb	turn at halfway	17 mins	20 mins
joint	per 448 g/1 lb [max 3.6 kg/4 lb]	place on plate	15 mins per 448 g	15 mins
steak	2x224 g/8 oz	turn over half-way	8–9 mins	5 mins
lamb chop	2x168 g/6 oz	turn over half-way	4 mins	1 min
pork chop	2x196 g/7 oz	turn over half-way	6–7	5 mins
bacon [rashers]	224 g/8 oz	separate slices	3 mins	
liver lambs/pig	224 g/8 oz	separate slices	5 mins	3 mins
kidney lambs	4	turn over half-way	3–4 mins	5 mins
mince beef	448 g/1 lb	break up meat halfway	15 mins	5 mins
beefburger	2		2 mins	
Sausage meat	224 g/8 oz	break up half-way	5 mins	2 mins
casserole	672 g/1^1/$_2$lb	separate with fork half-way	10 mins	10 mins

COOKING CHARTS
Vegetables

Vegetable	Amount	Cooking Time	Standing Time	Method
Asparagus	448 g/1 lb	7-8 mins	2 mins	covered dish – add 30 ml/2 tbs water
Broad Beans	448 g/1 lb	12 mins	2 mins	covered dish – add 60 ml/4 tbs water
French Beans	448 g/1 lb whole beans	8 mins	2 mins	covered dish – add 60 ml/4 tbs water
Runner Beans	448 g/1 lb sliced	7 mins	2 mins	covered dish – add 60 ml/4 tbs water
Broccoli	448 g/1 lb	9-10 mins	4 mins	covered dish – add 60 ml/4 tbs water
Cabbage	448 g/1 lb shredded	9–11 mins	4 mins	covered dish – add 45 ml/3 tbs water
Carrots	448 g/1 lb cut into 1.5 cm/^{1}/$_2$ in slices	9–10 mins	2 mins	covered dish – add 30 ml/2 tbs water
Cauliflower	448 g/1 lb broken into pieces	9–11 mins	2 mins	covered dish – add 60 ml/4 tbs water
Courgettes	448 g/1 lb sliced	4 mins	6 mins	cooking bag – add 28 g/ 1 oz butter

Vegetable	Amount	Cooking Time	Standing Time	Method
Leeks	448 g/1 lb sliced	8–9 mins	2 mins	covered dish – add 28 g/1 oz butter
Mushrooms	224 g/8 oz	3 mins	2 mins	covered shallow dish – add 28g/1 oz butter and dash of lemon
Onions	224 g/8 oz	4 mins	2 mins	covered dish
Parsnips	448 g/1 lb sliced	8–10 mins	2 mins	covered dish add boiling, 45 ml/3 tbs water
Peas	448 g/1 lb	6–8 mins	2 mins	cooking bag – add 45 ml/3 tbs water
Potatoes boiled	448 g/1 lb even sizes	10—12 mins	3 mins	covered dish – add 60 ml/4 tbs; water serve with butter
mashed	448 g/1 lb cut into small pieces	9–10 mins	3 mins	covered dish – add 60 ml/4 tbs water; add a little butter 3 tbs milk season well and mash
baked	2 potatoes 168 g/6 oz each	6 mins	4 mins	prick with fork 4/5 times and put on kitchen paper
Spinach	448 g/1 lb	6–7 mins	2 mins	covered dish
Swede turnip	448 g/1 lb – cubed	10–12 mins	2 mins	covered dish, add 45 ml/3 tbs water

Poultry

Type	Weight	Cooking Time	Standing Time	Method
Chicken portions	per 448 g/1 lb	7 mins	3 mins	season with chicken seasoning; place thin area towards centre and cover
Turkey	per 448 g/1 lb	12 mins per 448 g power 7	20 minutes covered in foil	brush with melted butter; sprinkle with seasoning; cover with bag or cling film; turn over and around 4 times basting well during cooking; shield wings and legs with foil
Roast Chicken/ Duck	per 448 g/1 lb	7 mins per 448 g	5 mins	as above when stuffing bird allow 5 mins extra
Boneless Roast Turkey	per 448 g/1 lb	12 mins per 448 g	15 mins covered in foil	put on plate; cover with cling film or see Hints and Tips on colour. Rotate twice during cooking

Meat

Type	Weight	Condition	Full Power	Half Power
Beef	below 1 kg/2 lb	rare	first 3 mins	7–8 mins per 448 g/1 lb
-	over 1 kg/2 lb	medium	first 6 mins	8–9 per 448 g/1 lb
-	–	well done	–	9-10 mins per 448 g/1 lb
Lamb	1 kg/2 lb (+ over)	well done	first 5 mins	9 mins per 448 g/1 lb
Veal	1 kg/2 lb (+ over)	well done	first 5 mins	9 mins per 448 g/1 lb
Pork	1 kg/2 lb (+ over)	well done	first 8 mins	10 mins per 448 g/1 lb

Any meat over 2 lbs use temperature probe

Rice

Type	Amount	Cooking Time	Standing Time	Method
long grain	224 g/ 8 oz	10–12 mins	3–4 mins	uncovered dish; add 900 ml/1^1/$_2$ pints cold water
brown	224 g/ 8 oz	20 mins full 8 mins half	3–4 mins	uncovered dish; add 900 ml/1^1/$_2$ pints boiling salted water
easy cook	224 g/8 oz	10 mins	3–4 mins	uncovered dish; add 600 ml/1 pint boiling salted water

Pasta

Type	Amount	Cooking Time	Standing Time	Method
spaghetti	224 g/8 oz	12 mins	3–4 mins	covered dish, 1.2 litres/2 pints boiling salted water and 15 ml/1 tbs oil
macaroni	224 g/8 oz	9 mins	3–4 mins	covered dish; 1.2 litres/2 pints boiling salted water and 15 ml/1 tbs oil
tagliatelli	224 g/8 oz	6 mins	3–4 mins	covered dish; 1.2 litres/2 pints boiling salted water and 15 ml/1 tbs oil
pasta shells	224 g/8 oz	8 mins	5–6 mins	covered dish; 1.2 litres/2 pints boiling salted water and 15 ml/1 tbs oil
lasagne	6-8 sheets	10 mins	5 mins	covered dish; 600–900 ml/1–1$^1/_2$ pints boiling salted water and 15 ml/1 tbs oil

Weights and Measures

American	Imperial	Metric
6 ml	1 teaspoon	5 ml
12 ml	1 tablespoon	15 ml
	1 oz	28 g
4 cups	1 lb	448g
2 cups	24 fl oz	600 ml
1 cup	12 fl oz	300 ml
1 cup	4 oz	112 g

Notes